Ein Heldenleben
Tone Poem for Orchestra
Op. 40

Richard Strauss

DOVER PUBLICATIONS, INC.
Mineola, New York

Bibliographical Note

This Dover edition, first published in 2002, is an unabridged republication of *Ein Heldenleben. Tondichtung für grosses Orchester von Richard Strauss, Op. 40*, originally published by the Verlag von F. E. C. Leuckart, Leipzig [1899; first edition]. Newly added lists of contents and instrumentation, a glossary of German performance indications, and footnote translations have been specially prepared by Stanley Appelbaum.

International Standard Book Number: 0-486-42441-3

Manufactured in the United States of America
Dover Publications, Inc., 31 East 2nd Street, Mineola, N.Y. 11501

CONTENTS

Dedicated to Wilhelm Mengelberg
and the Amsterdam Concertgebouw Orchestra

EIN HELDENLEBEN
(A Hero's Life)
Tone Poem for Orchestra
Op. 40

Composed 1898

First performed:
3 March 1899, Frankfurt am Main

Although "A Hero's Life" is the universally accepted English translation of *Ein Heldenleben,* the title is more accurately rendered as "A Heroic Life." Traditional program notes for this work incorporate subtitles said to have originated with the composer: "The Hero" . . . "The Hero's Adversaries" . . . "The Hero's Helpmate" . . ." "The Hero's Battlefield". . . "The Hero's Work of Peace" . . . "The Hero's Escape from the World and His Fulfillment." However, Leukart's first edition of the full score (1899)—the basis for the present Dover edition and almost certainly supervised by Strauss himself— carries no such subtitles.

INSTRUMENTATION

Piccolo [kleine Flöte, kl. Fl.]
3 Flutes [grosses Flöten, gr. Fl.]
4 Oboes [Oboen]
    Oboe IV doubles English Horn [engl. Horn]
$E\flat$ Clarinet [Es Clar.]
2 Clarinets in $B\flat$ [Clar. (B)]
Bass Clarinet in $B\flat$ [Bassclar. (B)]
3 Bassoons [Fagotte]
Contrabassoon [Contrafag(ott)]

8 Horns in E, F [Hörner, Hör.]
5 Trumpets in $E\flat$, $B\flat$ [Tromp(t). (Es, B)]
3 Trombones [Posaunen]
Tenor Tuba in $B\flat$ [Tenortuba (B)]
Bass Tuba [Basstuba]

Timpani [Pauke(n)]
Percussion
    Bass Drum [gr(osse) Trommel]
    Cymbals [Becken]
    Small Snare Drum (high) [kl(eine) Militärtr(ommel) (hoch)]
    Large Tenor Drum [gr(osse) Rührtr(ommel)]

2 Harps [Harfe(n)]

Violins I, II [Violinen, Viol.] (16 + 16)
Violas [Bratschen] (12)
Cellos [Violonc(ell)] (12)
Basses [Contrab(ässe)] (8)

Ein Heldenleben.

Tondichtung für großes Orchester

von

Richard Strauss.

Op. 40.   Partitur.   Pr. netto M 36,—

GLOSSARY OF GERMAN PERFORMANCE
INDICATIONS WITHIN THE SCORE

alle: all of them play; *alle übrigen:* all the rest; *allmählich etwas fliessender:* gradually more flowing; *allmählich immer ruhiger:* growing gradually calmer; *allmählich im Zeitmass etwas steigern:* quicken the tempo gradually; *allmählich nachlassen:* slacken gradually; *allmählich wieder lebhafter:* gradually more lively again; *ausdrucksvoll:* expressively; *aushalten!!:* prolong the note!!; *Becken gewöhnlich:* cymbals played the usual way; *beinahe doppelt so langsam (schnell):* nearly twice as slowly (fast); *beruhigend:* calming down; . . . *bis—fest im gewonnenen, lebhaften Zeitmass:* until attaining a lively tempo, then steady; *Dämpfer weg:* remove mute; . . . *des vorigen Zeitmasses:* . . . of the foregoing tempo; *die Hälfte:* half of them play; *die übrigen:* the others (the rest); *doppelt so schnell:* twice as fast; *drängend (und immer heftiger):* with urgency (and more and more violently); *dreifach:* in three parts; *Erstes Zeitmass:* first tempo; *Es:* E-flat; *etwas breit(er):* somewhat (more) broadly; *Etwas langsamer:* somewhat more slowly; *etwas markirt:* somewhat marcato; *Festes Zeitmass:* steady tempo; *gedämpft:* muted; *gestopft:* stopped notes; *Ges wieder nach G umstimmen:* tune G-flat back to G again; *geteilt (pultweise):* divided (by desks); *getragen:* sustained; *G nach Ges herunterstimmen:* tune G down to G-flat; *Heftig bewegt:* with violent agitation; *hervortretend:* prominently; *heuchlerisch schmachtend:* hypocritically languishing; *hinter der Scene:* offstage; *hoch:* high; *immer langsamer:* more and more slowly; *immer ruhiger:* more and more calmly; *immer schneller und rasender:* more and more rapidly and wildly; *im Orchester:* in the orchestra; *im Zeitmass:* in tempo; *kräftig, heiter:* powerfully, humorously; *lange Pause:* long rest; *Langsam:* slowly; *lebhaft:* lively; *Lebhaft bewegt:* with lively motion; *leicht beschwingt:* lightly soaring; *leichtfertig:* frivolously; *liebenswürdig:* amiably; *lustig:* merrily; *Mässig langsam:* moderately slowly; *mit Dämpfer(n):* with mute(s); *mit grossem Schwung (und Begeisterung):* with great zest (and enthusiasm); *mit Holzschlägel(n):* with (a) wooden stick(s); *mit Steigerung:* with intensification; *nicht abdämpfen:* do not mute; *nicht geteilt:* not divided; *ohne Dämpfer:* without mute; *plötzlich wieder ruhig und sehr gefühlvoll:* suddenly calm again and very affectionately; *Pult:* desk; *Saite:* string; *schnarrend:* rasping; *schnell und keifend:* fast and naggingly; *sehr ausdrucksvoll:* very expressively; *sehr energisch:* very energetically; *sehr getragen:* very sustained; *sehr lebhaft:* very lively; *sehr ruhig:* very calmly; *sehr scharf (und spitzig):* very sharply (and pointedly); *Solobratsche:* solo viola; *Soloviol[ine]:* solo violin; *spielend:* playfully; *träumend:* dreamily; *übermütig:* in high spirits; *viel bewegter:* much more agitatedly; *viel lebhafter:* much more lively; *viel ruhiger:* much more calmly; *vierfach:* in four parts; *voll Sehnsucht:* full of longing; *vom 1. Pult:* from the first desk; *weich:* gently; *Wieder (etwas) langsamer (ruhiger):* (somewhat) more slowly (calmly) again; *wieder lebhaft:* lively again; *wieder sehr ruhig:* very calmly again; *wie ganz von ferne:* as if from a great distance; *zart(,) ausdrucksvoll:* with tender expression; *zart, etwas sentimental:* tenderly, somewhat sentimentally; *zart hervortretend:* tenderly standing out; *zart und liebevoll:* tenderly and lovingly; *ziemlich lebhaft:* fairly lively; *zischend:* hissing; *zornig:* angrily; *zurückhaltend:* holding back; *zweifach:* in two parts.

1

6

12

18

25

*) ～ bedeutet: von einem Ton zum andern schleifen (portamento)

[This sign indicates *portamento* between tones.]

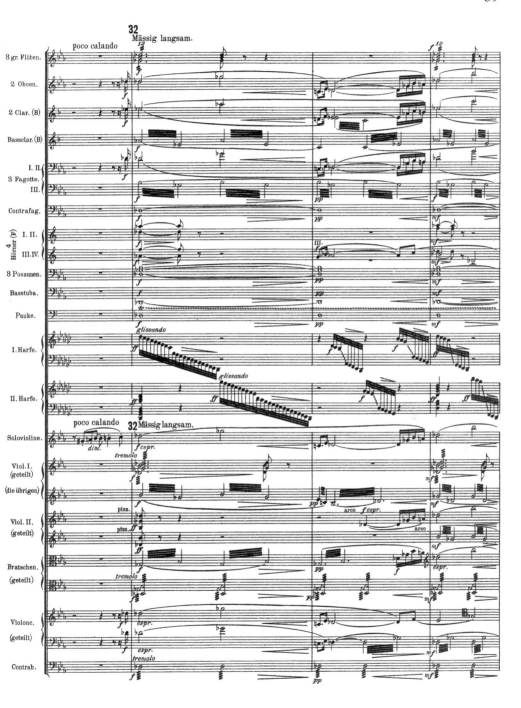

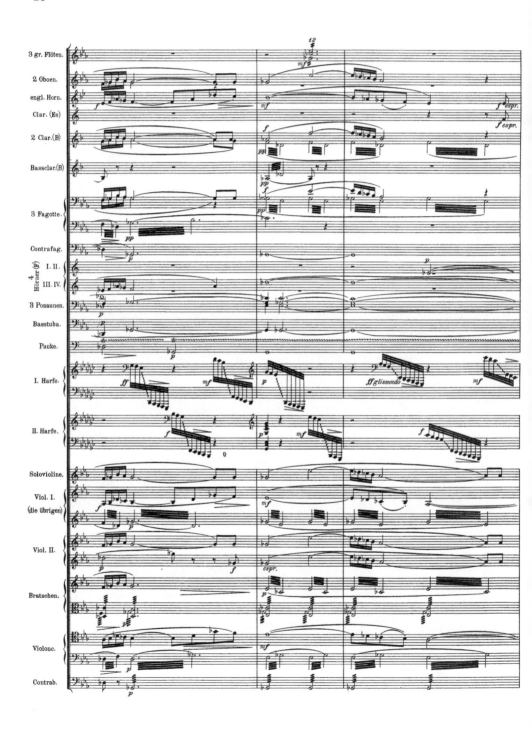

42

★) mit springendem Bogen.

[spiccato]

116

118

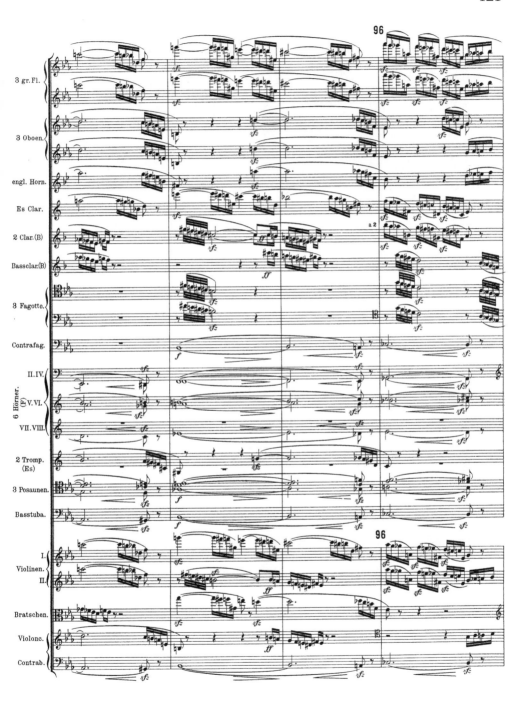

124

136

Berlin - Charlottenburg 27.Dezember 1898.

Ende.